Stop Living Broke

Sista Jay Jay

(Dr. JoeDrell Benjamin)

DEDICATION

I dedicate this book to everyone who has been trapped by a poverty mentality—those who have been taught to settle for less, to believe lack is normal, or to live in cycles of survival instead of abundance. This book is for you. May it open your eyes to new possibilities, break limiting beliefs, and inspire you to step boldly into financial freedom, mental wealth, and a richer life.

CONTENTS

ACKNOWLEDGMENTS

First, I give honor to God, the source of my strength, vision, and perseverance. Without His grace, none of this would be possible.

To my family—thank you for your love, patience, and encouragement through every late night, every draft, and every challenge. Your belief in me has been my anchor.

To my network of friends, mentors, and collaborators—your wisdom, accountability, and inspiration have kept me focused and fueled my drive. Thank you for helping me to prove that "collaboration over competition" truly builds lasting success.

To the readers of this book—I see you, I believe in you, and I wrote these words for you. If you've ever felt trapped by limitations, weighed down by a poverty mindset, or afraid that life would never change, know this: your story is not over. You hold the power to break cycles, to create wealth, and to live a life of freedom and purpose.

Finally, to every dreamer who refuses to quit, every believer who dares to rise, and every ordinary person determined to create extraordinary results—this book is for you. May it spark courage, awaken vision, and help you step into the rich, full life you were created to live.

CHAPTER ONE
The Shift

I can recall a time in my life that I was so broke that if someone would've tried to rob me, it would have just been practice.

The stories I could talk about, being in an unhealthy financial position would have you laughing and shaking your head, while also feeling the weight of empathy.

Here's one.

It was back-to-school time, and I had blown money on things that didn't even matter. When it came time to buy my son new shoes, my pockets were nearly empty. He had grown used to the latest Jordans—the kind that dropped monthly—and I made sure he had a new pair every single time. But then the storm came. Bills piled up, due dates came faster than paychecks, and I couldn't keep up.

The kids began to notice the shift. No more trips to Mickey D's whenever they wanted. No more fresh sneakers or new clothes at the snap of a finger. So, when school rolled around, I wanted my then only son to settle for a pair of black-and-white high-top, low-grade Nikes. I'll never forget his reaction—he was livid. Instead of sitting him down to explain, I lashed out and called him ungrateful. The truth was, I wasn't angry at him. I was angry at myself.

Here's another one—this one is harder to admit.

I was working as a hairstylist at the time, and money was flowing. I was making good money with my hands every day, yet somehow, I was still broke. I was still in need. I was still struggling to keep food on the table. And yes, despite the income, I was on food stamps.

That was an all-time low for me. Not just financially, but emotionally. Looking back, it wasn't the lack of money that broke me—it was the lack of control, the lack of discipline, and the lack of truth.

I could go on and on entertaining you with my crazy yet unhealthy financial stories, but it wasn't until years later, that I had my epiphany.

It was raining outside, hard. I had just finished putting my now second son to bed. (The other children were young adults, some in college others in the working world. I was now a divorcee.) The home was finally quiet, but I was anything but calm. My body was tired, but my mind was louder than ever. I walked to the kitchen and checked my bank account. $3.29. Rent was due. That number burned into my brain like a scar.

Unfortunately, that wasn't the first time I had seen my account that low, but it was the first time it made me *stop*. I stood there at my kitchen table, hands trembling, thinking, *This can't be my life*. I was working and doing stage plays, writing books, making money, giving my all to everyone around me, and still—I was drowning. *I knew the life I led before was not an option. Although, it kept crossing my mind.* I was at my end. It was just me and my son. I felt as if I couldn't turn to anyone in my family for help because they all thought I was doing great. I resided in a good county. My son had just transition from private school to the county public school. I lived in a luxury apartment. I drove a nice car. My youngest son was always well-kept, and I stayed looking amazing. I always appeared to have it all together because I made sure everyone knew it. I needed them to know that I wasn't trying to be like the Joneses, I was the Joneses. But secretly, life was hitting me hard, and I needed to make some decisions. But first I had to admit something to myself.

I was living broke.

I reached into a drawer and pulled out a blank notebook. I opened it to the first page and wrote, "I need to change." That moment—simple as it was—was the beginning of me taking back the wheel of my life. I no longer wanted to live broke.

Let me tell you something that I've learned the hard way: If you don't put yourself first, life will keep putting you last. I spent years trying to be everything for everyone else. Mother. Daughter. Employee. Friend. I wore those labels like a badge of honor, but inside, I was crumbling. It wasn't until I put myself first—my *health*, my *peace*, my *finances*—that things started to change.

Here's the truth most people don't talk about: nobody is coming to save you. Not your boss. Not your partner. Not the government. You have to save yourself. And that starts with making a decision—one decision—to take back control.

When I had a fainting spell at work from exhaustion, the doctor called it fatigue. But I called it my wake-up call. My best friend at the time told me, "This isn't living, Jay. This is slow death." And she was right. That conversation planted a seed.

I started waking up ten minutes earlier each day. Just ten minutes. I didn't check my phone or my emails. I just sat. I asked myself one question: "What do I want?" Not what my kids needed. Not what my mom expected. Not what my job demanded. *What do I want?*

I wrote it down on a piece of paper: **Peace.**

That word became my compass.

From that point on, every decision I made had to align with peace. If it didn't bring me closer to peace—financially, emotionally, or mentally—I let it go. Saying no became my new superpower. No to unnecessary things that drained my energy but didn't move me forward. No to toxic conversations that kept me stuck in negativity. No to hanging out just because folks knew I would take the check and when I did go out only paying my bill. No to guilt that made me feel like I owed everyone but myself. No to weekend shopping sprees.

True story: My younger sister and I went to the mall not long after I had committed to my new financial habits. We had only been there about 30 minutes when I noticed the difference between us. She was spending, buying, spending, buying—bag after bag. Meanwhile, I picked up just a few small things, but the pressure around me started to feel overwhelming.

The temptation was so strong that I eventually had to walk away. I left her in the mall and went to sit in my car. As soon as I closed the door, my chest got tight, and I began to hyperventilate. I sat there, breathing, reflecting on how close I had come to slipping back into my old ways—

spending money carelessly and neglecting my financial obligations, just like I had done so many times before.

But then something shifted. I calmed myself down and began to speak encouragement over myself. I reminded myself of why I had started this journey and the future I was building. And in that moment, I realized something important: **I have to make decisions that are best for me and for the future me and I was okay with that.**

At first, people didn't like the new me. Some resisted, some fell away, and others didn't understand. But what I gained was far more valuable than their approval: I gained space. Space to think. Space to feel. Space to breathe. For the first time in years, I wasn't running on autopilot. I was making choices that honored my future instead of sabotaging it.

With that new clarity, I began to lean into learning. I started listening to podcasts on personal finance. I picked up books that challenged my mindset. I worked on my portfolio, and I finally sat down with my numbers face to face. It was humbling. It was uncomfortable. But it was also powerful—because for the first time, I wasn't hiding from the truth.

That process exposed something I had been avoiding: I was an emotional spender. I bought takeout when I was tired. I bought clothes, jewelry, hair units, expensive perfumes without a second thought. I bought little comforts to make up for big frustrations. And though each purchase seemed harmless in the moment, they added up in ways that kept me stuck.

That's when awareness became my greatest weapon. Awareness forced me to see my money patterns for what they were—not random, not accidental, but emotional. Once I saw it, I could no longer deny it. And that awareness gave me the power to begin changing it.

Let's take a look at awareness and the role it plays in financial freedom.

Awareness is the first step to financial freedom because you cannot change what you refuse to acknowledge. Too many people live in a fog when it comes to money. They know bills are due, but they don't know the total. They swipe their cards, but they don't track the balance. They feel broke, but they can't explain where their money is actually going. That lack of awareness keeps them stuck in cycles of stress, debt, and frustration.

When I finally sat down with my numbers, it was like turning on the lights in a dark room. At first, it was uncomfortable. I saw things I didn't want to see—bank fees, overdrafts, wasted spending on things that didn't even matter to me long term. But as painful as it was, it was also freeing. For the first time, I had clarity. I could see the truth, and the truth gave me power.

Awareness stops you from lying to yourself. It forces you to admit that $10 a day on fast food isn't just a harmless habit—it's $300 a month that could have been invested, saved, or used to pay down debt. It forces you to see that "just one more subscription" is harmless especially when it's multiplied by six or seven more subscriptions. It forces you to recognize that being broke isn't just about not having money—it's about how you handle the money you do have.

That's why awareness is such a game-changer. It shifts you from being a victim of money to being a manager of money. It allows you to make intentional choices instead of emotional ones. It shows you where you are so you can chart a course to where you want to be.

Here's a true story: I was once married. My then husband never wanted to sit down and have honest conversations about money. At first, I was okay with it, because I felt like he trusted me and that I was in control. I convinced myself that handling the bills and managing the budget on my own was a sign of responsibility, maybe even strength. But over time, that "control" became a heavy burden.

He left all the bill paying, budgeting, and financial planning to me, while swiping the card at will. It didn't matter if the account was healthy or hanging by a thread—he spent without thought or discussion. And when the account was low or even overdrawn, the blame would always find its way back to me.

We argued constantly about his lack of discipline and careless spending habits. I tried to set boundaries. I tried to create systems. I even scheduled "Money Monday" meetings at the beginning of each month so we could sit down together, review the bills, and create a plan. But instead of leaning into partnership, he resisted. He would deliberately start arguments on those days, turning what should have been a time of alignment into an exhausting battle. It was emotionally draining, financially stressful, and deeply frustrating.

Over time, I began to see the pattern clearly: avoidance. As long as he could shift the blame to me, he never had to face his own financial choices. As long as he stirred up conflict, he never had to confront the numbers. But here's the reality—avoiding the truth never fixes the problem. It only delays the inevitable and deepens the damage.

Those experiences taught me something important: money is never just about money. It's about values, discipline, partnership, and communication. When one person refuses to take responsibility, the weight falls on the other, and resentment grows. Financial stress doesn't just affect your bank account—it seeps into your peace, your relationships, and your future.

That season of my life was exhausting, yes, but it was also eye-opening. It showed me how vital it is to not only manage money but to also manage the mindset and habits around money. Because without awareness, accountability, consistency, and respect for the plan, financial freedom will always feel out of reach.

The bottom line about awareness is that you cannot *stop living broke* until you know exactly why you're broke. Awareness is the bridge between ignorance and action, between excuses and accountability. Once you become aware, you can no longer hide—and that's the moment transformation begins.

Once I accepted awareness about how I was handling money, something beautiful happened. My youngest son looked at me one day and asked, "Ma Dukes, why do you smile more now?"

My answer: "Because I'm aware."

Let's be clear: this journey wasn't about a fancy budget or a trendy vision board. It was about waking up from survival mode and realizing I deserved better. It was about confronting a mindset I didn't even know I had—the mindset of lack, of fear, of waiting on someone else to fix what I had the power to change.

You see, poverty isn't just a bank balance. It's a belief system. A belief that you're not worthy of more, that you have to hustle until you collapse, that money is always scarce. It's the voice that says, "This is just how it is for people like us."

But that voice lies.

I watched members of my family work their fingers to the bone, refusing to listen to the wise counsel of those who let their money work for them. From childhood, I realized that I didn't want that kind of life. I didn't want to work just to be exhausted, or to work endlessly only to stay broke. I refused to accept that seed of struggle as my destiny.

As I began to educate myself, I saw that:

- You don't have to earn your worth through exhaustion.

- You don't have to prove you're deserving by struggling.
- You are allowed to want more. To need more. To become more.
- And here's the part that freed me: you don't have to apologize for it.

The first step in shifting out of a poor mentality is believing that you can. Because if you don't believe it's possible, you won't fight for it. That belief becomes your fuel. Once I truly believed I was capable of change, my actions started to match that belief.

And it's not about big, dramatic moves. It's about simple, daily choices. Saying no to spending out of boredom. Saying yes to reading that free financial guide instead of watching another show. Choosing water over soda. Walking instead of scrolling. Every little shift matters. That's how you build momentum. I know because that's how I built my momentum.

When you shift from survival to strategy, everything begins to change. You stop reacting and start planning.

You stop begging and start building. You stop sacrificing your future for temporary comfort.

That's why putting yourself first isn't selfish. It's *strategic*. Because when you're well—mentally, emotionally, and financially—you're stronger. Wiser. Clearer. And when you're clear, you make better choices. You see through the fog. You break the cycle.

I want you to know something: You are not lazy. You are not broken. You are not too far gone. You've just been in survival mode too long. And it's time to shift.

This chapter is the foundation. It's about reclaiming your right to exist beyond the grind. It's about understanding that your mindset is the steering wheel, and your choices are the engine.

Every time you choose peace over chaos, growth over fear, clarity over confusion—you take back the wheel.

And this is just the beginning.

CHAPTER TWO
Understanding Money-From Survival to Strategy

If Chapter One was about reclaiming your life, Chapter Two is about reclaiming your money. Because whether we like it or not, money touches every part of our lives. It affects our health, our relationships, our sleep, and even our self-worth.

Let me be honest—I used to have a horrible relationship with money. Not because I didn't want to be responsible, but because no one ever taught me how. I grew up hearing things like "money doesn't grow on trees" and "we can't afford that." And slowly, those phrases shaped my beliefs. I believed that being broke was just part of the deal. I believed struggle made me stronger. Through life's journey, I was made to believe that If I wanted more than what I had was me wanting someone else's life and that made me ungrateful and even greedy. So not true. But here's what I finally learned: poverty is not a character trait. It's a circumstance—and more importantly, it's one you can change.

I had to stop treating money like an enemy. I had to get honest about my habits. When I finally sat down and looked at my spending, I realized I wasn't struggling because I didn't make enough. I was struggling because I didn't have a plan. I was reacting to life instead of running it like a business.

So, I started small. I started my budgeting excel sheet. I tracked every dollar for 30 days. I watched every dollar like a hawk. I looked at my subscriptions. I looked at my eating-out habits. I looked at the emotional spending I used to fill holes in my life that I didn't focus on before.

That first month, I saved over $250 just by being aware.

Let that sink in. It may not seem like a lot but that was money that I was able to keep in my account and that is a major win any time I can save money.

Money isn't about math. It's about mindset. And until you change your mindset, your money will keep slipping through your fingers like water.

I learned to give every dollar a job. I stopped swiping my card without thinking. I made rules for myself. I created a goal: build an emergency fund (I'm not sharing my amount because should you choose to do the same, I do not want my goal to interfere with you making the goal that is best for you.) It took me two months. That emergency fund changed everything. Not just because it was money in the bank—but because it was *proof* that I could do this.

If you're reading this and feel buried in debt, know this: you're not alone. According to a 2024 financial report, over 60% of Americans live paycheck to paycheck. Most people on a middle class or lower financial status don't even have $400 saved for an emergency. So, if you're in this place, don't feel ashamed—feel motivated.

This is where your shift from survival to strategy begins.

Here are five truths I wish someone had told me earlier:

1. **You don't have a money problem. You have a strategy problem.**

2. **Budgeting isn't about restriction. It's about direction.**

3. **You can out-earn your excuses, but only if you're honest with yourself.**

4. **Debt is not a life sentence. It's a battle you can win.**

5. **You deserve financial peace, no matter where you started.**

Changing your money habits doesn't require perfection. It requires consistency. Financial growth isn't about never making a mistake, never splurging, or never stumbling— it's about showing up day after day with intentional choices that move you forward.

Consistency looks like checking your bank account regularly, so you know where your money is going instead of being blindsided at the end of the month. It looks like setting spending limits that protect you from impulse decisions. It looks like creating a grocery list before you walk into the store, so you shop with discipline instead of distraction.

It also means delaying gratification for greater gain. Instead of chasing the temporary thrill of the latest purchase, you train yourself to find joy in saving, investing, and building. That doesn't mean you can't ever enjoy life—but it means you refuse to trade your long-term security for short-term pleasure.

Over time, these small decisions compound. Each budget you follow, each unnecessary purchase you avoid, each dollar you set aside is a brick in the foundation of your financial freedom. You may not see the results overnight, but consistency will always outwork perfection.

So, stop waiting for the "perfect" moment to start. Start where you are, with what you have, and commit to progress over perfection. Because when it comes to money, consistency is the quiet force that turns broke habits into wealthy habits—and eventually, into a lifestyle of freedom.

Be consistent, build wisely, and stop living broke.

Let's talk about what I call the "Financial Reset Plan":

1. Track Everything – For one full month, write down every single dollar you spend. Use a notebook, spreadsheet, or app. This isn't about guilt—it's about awareness.

2. Know Your Numbers – List all your bills, debt, income, and subscriptions. It might be scary, but clarity brings control. If you're afraid to look at your bank account, ask yourself why. Shame thrives in silence.

3. Create a Simple Budget – Start with what's called the 50/30/20 rule: 50% of your income goes to needs, 30% to wants, 20% to savings and debt. Adjust to fit your reality. Even if you can only save 5%, start there. *Remember: the habit matters more than the amount.*

4. Build an Emergency Fund – Start small and then build to at least $1,000. This gives you room to breathe and stops the cycle of panic when life throws curveballs. One flat tire won't derail your life. That kind of buffer is freedom.

5. Attack Your Debt – Use either the "snowball method" (smallest debt first) or the "avalanche method" (highest interest rate first). Momentum is key. Seeing a balance hit zero does more for your motivation than any financial lecture ever could. I know because I felt that motivation each time a credit card or bill was paid.

And here's the most important part: It's okay to ask for help.

I watched financial podcasts and read books on money until the concepts started to sink in. I didn't just want to make money—I wanted to understand it. I wanted to know how it worked, how it grew, and how wealthy people thought differently about it. I studied the way they made decisions, the risks they took, and the habits they built.

Books like *Rich Dad Poor Dad* and *A Happy Pocket Full of Money* opened my mind to new ways of thinking. They challenged me to stop looking at money as something scarce and start seeing it as something that flows—a resource that grows when it's respected, not feared.

I went deeper than just tips and tricks. I researched the very concept of money itself—the value it carries, the history behind it, and how societies have always used it as a tool of exchange, power, and freedom. The more I studied, the more I realized that money has always been about belief, discipline, and systems. When you respect those principles, money works for you. When you ignore them, money works against you.

I also began following people on social media who taught money with heart, not just formulas. People who didn't just talk about spreadsheets and stock charts, but about mindset, vision, and purpose. They reminded me that wealth isn't just about numbers—it's about building a life of freedom, peace, and impact. And slowly, something shifted. My financial confidence grew. I stopped feeling like money was this mysterious, intimidating thing that controlled me, and I began to feel empowered to take control of it. Each book, each podcast, each piece of research added another layer to my understanding. I realized that financial freedom isn't built overnight—it's built one lesson, one shift, one action at a time.

I stopped thinking of money as something to fear and started seeing it for what it truly is—a tool. Money was never meant to be a master. It's not the enemy, and it's not the answer to everything. It's simply a tool. A tool to create the life I wanted. A tool to heal from past struggles by building stability. A tool to breathe a little easier because bills no longer controlled every thought. A tool to dream bigger without the constant weight of "how will I afford it?" hanging over my head.

When I shifted my perspective, I realized that money doesn't define me—it serves me. That change in mindset gave me the power to stop running from financial responsibility and start taking control of it. And that's where freedom begins; not with a million dollars in the bank, but with a renewed relationship with money.

Here's the truth: financial stress is emotional stress. According to the American Psychological Association, over 70% of adults report money as a significant source of stress. That kind of weight affects your mental health, your relationships, and even your physical health. It's time we stop treating financial education like an optional skill. Understand, we need the knowledge to develop our financial strategies. Let's talk about financial trauma for a moment-the kind passed down generationally. The fear of not having enough. The fear of losing it all. The belief that wealth is "for other people." Many of us are the first in our families to even *think* about building wealth. That's not just financial work—it's emotional labor.

And guess what? You're strong enough to do it.

When you start to get control of your money, something powerful happens: you begin to dream again. The fog of stress and fear starts to lift, and for the first time in a long time, you can see possibilities. You start making plans— not just for the week ahead, but for the future you once thought was out of reach. Suddenly, it feels good to save. It feels empowering to say no to a purchase that doesn't align with your values. And each small decision becomes a building block in the life you're creating.

You begin to realize that you're not just surviving anymore—you're living. You're choosing with intention instead of reacting with desperation. You're stepping out of cycles that once held you captive, and you're building new habits that strengthen your confidence and expand your vision. This is the moment when financial control shifts from being a burden to being a gift.

Don't let anyone tell you financial freedom isn't for you. It is. It's not reserved for the wealthy, the privileged, or the lucky—it's available to anyone willing to take ownership, face the truth, and do the work. And it starts the moment you stop hiding from your money and start leading it.

Make yourself a promise: No more silence. No more shame. No more pretending. Your financial journey is not about guilt—it's about growth. Every step you take is proof that you are not just fixing your finances—you are rewriting your future.

In the next chapter, we'll talk about something just as powerful—asking for help. You don't have to do any of this alone.

CHAPTER THREE
The Strength in Surrender

"Closed mouths don't get fed." That saying is so true. Think about it—how can a doctor help you if you never tell them what's wrong? In order to receive help, you must first acknowledge that there is a need.

The challenge is, many people would rather continue stumbling down a dark path, hoping they'll eventually find light, than simply ask for help. Why? Sometimes it's pride. Sometimes it's fear of being judged. Sometimes it's the feeling of inadequacy—the lie that if you ask for help, people will think you're weak, stupid, or incapable. But let's call it what it is: pride comes before destruction. What's truly inadequate is choosing to function in disarray. And what's truly foolish is refusing to ask for help when help is available.

This is another reason why so many people remain broke—not just financially, but mentally and emotionally. They have broken behaviors. They carry habits of silence, shame, and stubbornness that keep them trapped. Instead of opening their mouths to seek wisdom, guidance, or mentorship, they stay stuck in the same cycles.

But here's the truth: wealth is not a one-size-fits-all formula. It doesn't look the same for everyone. For one person, wealth may mean building a business. For another, it may mean being debt-free with peace of mind. For someone else, it may mean having enough investments to create generational security. The path to wealth is unique, but the first step for everyone is the same—acknowledging you need help, being willing to learn, and breaking free from broken behaviors. And that means having the strength to surrender into a better way of living.

Again, for some, wealth looks like luxury cars, designer clothes, and big houses. There's nothing wrong with those things—but that's not the only version of abundance.

For others, wealth looks like freedom. The freedom to rest. To wake up when your body says it's time. To take a walk with your kids. To be present. To have options.

I used to think wealth meant appearing successful. Having things that made me look like I had made it. But the more

I healed, the more I asked for help, the more I realized: *true wealth is peace.*

True wealth is knowing your bills are paid and your heart is light. It's not being afraid to answer the phone because of the fear of creditors. It's not losing sleep over rent. It's having a fridge with food, a plan for your future, and people who check on you not just when they need something, but because they genuinely care.

And when we teach ourselves—and the next generation—to value that kind of wealth, we shift everything. We teach our children to chase freedom, not debt. To honor joy over image. To build a life rooted in meaning, not just money.

So, before we move on, I want to ask you: *What does wealth mean to you?* Not what the world told you. Not what social media shows you. Not what your pride demands.

Ask yourself: *What would a wealthy life feel like?*

Would it feel calm? Would it feel safe? Would it feel free?

Define it for yourself. Write it down. And let that be your vision, your North Star. Because when we define wealth on our own terms, we stop competing and start creating. We stop comparing and start becoming.

Let's redefine success so that future generations don't inherit stress masked as success. Let's teach them that it's okay to want more—but only if it means more freedom, more rest, more joy, more love.

Because that, my friend, is the kind of wealth that doesn't just fill pockets—it fills hearts.

And here's something we must face head-on: people with a poor mentality often confuse *symbols* of wealth with actual wealth. They chase cars, clothes, and gadgets— things that lose value the moment they leave the store— because they've been taught that status equals success. It's not their fault. Many were raised in environments where survival was the priority, and appearances were the only form of social proof and acceptance.

But here's the hard truth: poor people often work to earn money just to stay in debt. Then they work even harder trying to get out of that debt. And once they do, they repeat the cycle—because the mindset hasn't changed.

A wealthy person thinks differently. A wealthy person asks, "How can I make my money work for me?" They invest. They buy assets, not liabilities. They value time over things, freedom over sparkles. They understand that buying something just to look successful is often what keeps people broke.

While poor-minded thinking sees a paycheck as permission to spend, wealthy-minded thinking sees a paycheck as a tool to grow. While poor thinking asks, "How much can I afford monthly?" wealth thinking asks, "Is this building my future?"

We must teach ourselves—and our children—that wealth isn't about showing off. It's about showing up for your life with intention. It's about choosing long-term peace over short-term pleasure.

We don't need to impress people. We need to free ourselves.

When you shift your thinking, you shift your reality. You stop working for money and start making money work for you. And that's when true freedom begins.

Let me give you two real-life examples that changed how I saw the world:

Example 1: Marcus and the Mercedes

Marcus (we will call him) was a co-worker of mine who always showed up looking polished. Fresh shoes, designer suits, and a brand-new Mercedes parked out front. To the outside world, Marcus was winning. But one day, during a slow moment at work, he admitted something that stunned me. He was drowning in debt. His car note was $780 a month, his credit cards were maxed out, and he was living paycheck to paycheck. He bought things to prove to others that he had made it—but inside, he felt trapped. "People respect the car," he said, "I get plenty of women and my boys love to ride in it, but they don't see the panic attacks I have every night."

Example 2: Brianna and the Basement

Then there was Brianna (again names are changed). She was quiet, low-key, and didn't dress flashy. Most folks underestimated her. But one day we got to talking and she revealed that she owned two rental properties and had zero debt. She still lived in her modest childhood home with her mom—by choice—because she was stacking her money. Her car was paid off, she used cash for everything, and she had built a six-month emergency fund. She had little followers on social media in fact she was barely on it. "I want freedom," she told me. "Not followers."

Those two conversations changed me. Marcus had the image. Brianna had the peace. And I realized: I wanted peace.

Let this be your wake-up call: You don't have to look rich to be wealthy. You don't have to keep buying things to prove your worth. Marcus was flexing but the real flexor was Brianna. She was flexing peace of mind, financial freedom, and generational change. Let's be clear. I'm not saying you can't look nice and have nice things or enjoy yourself. Just don't go broke doing so.

Choose wisely.

Let's take it deeper.

Marcus wasn't a bad person, and it could be argued that he wasn't irresponsible. He was doing what so many of us are conditioned to do: survive the trauma of poverty by trying to escape it with appearances. He once told me he remembered being teased for his worn-out sneakers in middle school. That embarrassment and trauma followed him into adulthood. So, when he finally started making good money, he promised himself he'd never look broke again—even if it meant going broke trying not to. Think about that for a moment. He was willing to go broke just not to look broke. But that's how unhealed trauma shows up financially.

On the surface, Marcus was 'winning.' But inside, he was at war with himself—working overtime to pay for things he didn't even have the time to enjoy. He was so busy chasing validation that he couldn't afford peace.

Now back to Brianna. She told me that her mom had been evicted when she was a kid, and they spent a year living with relatives. That instability scared her so much, she became obsessed with security. So, every dollar she made became a soldier—assigned to protect her future. While others were upgrading their lifestyles, she was upgrading her net worth. While Marcus was swiping cards to be seen, Brianna was investing in stocks, savings, and real estate— quietly building a life that couldn't be taken away.

That's the difference in mentality. One spent to feel like something because he remembered how it felt to feel like nothing. While the other saved because she remembered what it felt like to have nothing so she made decisions that would always allow her to have something.

This isn't just about money—it's about healing. Healing from the need to prove yourself. Healing from the pressure to keep up. Healing from a system that profits off your insecurity, past trauma and lack of financial literacy.

When you don't know who you are, you'll try to buy identity. When you don't feel worthy, you'll overspend trying to feel important. But when you heal; you start choosing what lasts and what has value and growth. You choose ownership over optics. You choose peace over performance.

And most of all—you choose yourself.

This is your invitation to pause. To reflect. To ask: *Why do I spend the way I spend? What am I trying to feel or fix?*

Understand that your relationship with money isn't just about dollars. It's about dignity.

Let's teach the next generation that real power isn't in what you wear—it's in what you own. It's in your choices. Your clarity. Your knowledge. Your freedom. Your joy. And your peace.

Let's leave them wealth that isn't just financial, but a balanced emotional and strategic mindset. Because true wealth doesn't shout. It whispers, *"You're safe now."* And you will know you're financially safe by the financial freedom you have.

And here's something even more important: **money should never define your value.**

You are not your salary. You are not your job title. You are not the brand of shoes on your feet or the kind of car you drive. Money is a tool—not a measure of your worth. And yet, so many of us have internalized the idea that we are only as valuable as what we earn or what we own.

That belief is dangerous. It keeps us in jobs that drain us. It makes us ashamed to ask for help. It pressures us to keep up appearances we can't afford and don't even enjoy. It tells us that unless we can show proof of success, we don't deserve respect.

But let me say this plainly: **you were valuable the day you were born.** Money can't add to that and losing it won't take it away.

The moment you stop letting your bank account dictate your self-worth, you free yourself from a powerful lie. You begin to make decisions from confidence, not comparison. From peace, not pressure.

You stop asking, "Do I have enough to matter?" and start declaring, "I matter, no matter what I have." That is shift in identity and that my friend is internal wealth.

Let's go even further.

We live in a world that teaches us early that our value is tied to what we produce or possess. Think about it: we praise kids for good grades and trophies. We praise adults for big salaries and promotions. From childhood, many of us learn that our worth is attached to material things—and earnings those things to gain a sense of worthiness often looks like exhaustion.

Many in the younger generation are turning away from traditional work because they have watched exhaustion consume their parents' lives. They see their parents labor endlessly, only to come home too tired to enjoy the fruits of their efforts. To them, work has become a trap—long hours traded for little reward.

Children grow up watching their parents miss milestones, family outings, and quality time—not because they don't care, but because they are worn down by the daily grind. In many households, the responsibility of caring for younger siblings falls on the eldest child. This creates a cycle of "children raising children," because parents are absent, either physically at work or emotionally drained.

The result is confusion and resentment. Children wonder how their parents can work so hard, yet still live paycheck to paycheck, always broke. They see sacrifice without reward, and they do not want to inherit that life. For them, this becomes a painful but powerful lesson: working without the purpose of a softer tomorrow or balance often leads to living broke.

Let's keep going.

When money is lacking, it's easy to believe we are lacking. When our pockets are empty, shame creeps in and tells us our soul is too. And that belief system—rooted in capitalism, trauma, and performance—becomes our identity.

That's why it's so important to challenge this lie: **Your value is not negotiable. It is not dependent on a number. It is not subject to your income bracket.**

Think about how many brilliant, creative, loving, resourceful people you know who are broke—not because they're broken in spirit, but because they've never had access to the tools or opportunities that allow their greatness to flourish. They are not less than. And neither are you. So do not equate lack of money with lack of a person's importance. Money is a tool that defines your financial growth and financial success. Who you are as a person defines your character and integrity. Both holds enormous worth.

We must be intentional about breaking this false connection between money and worth. Because if we don't, we will always hustle for approval. We will overwork, overspend, and overcompensate to feel like we belong in rooms we were already worthy to walk into.

Wealthy thinking is not just about having more money— it's about knowing that your value is consistent. It's the refusal to let numbers define your enoughness (yes I said enoughness). It's the quiet strength of a person who knows that their purpose is not tied to their paycheck.

So, the next time you start to measure your worth by your financial status, stop. Breathe and remind yourself: "My bank account can change. My job can change. But who I am? That doesn't change. I was born enough, and I still am worthy."

That's where true confidence begins. That's where true healing begins. And that's where real wealth begins—not in your wallet, but in your mind and in your heart.

Before I close this chapter, I want to leave you with this:

You have the power to be mentally wealthy before you're ever financially wealthy.

Let that sink in.

Mental wealth is the foundation on which every other kind of wealth is built. It's not just about being smart—it's about being grounded, clear, and whole on the inside. It means having the mindset of abundance, even when the bank account hasn't caught up yet. It means walking with vision and making choices that reflect your belief in your future.

People often wait until they "have money" to start feeling powerful. But power starts with your perspective. Mental wealth is waking up and deciding, "I matter. My future matters. My choices matter."

It's not about what you drive—it's about where you're going. It's not about the brand on your back—it's about the boldness in your spirit. It's not about how much is in your wallet—it's about how much you believe in yourself when everything is telling you not to.

If you begin to see yourself as already wealthy in discipline, focus, clarity, and purpose, your bank account will eventually catch up. Because money follows mindset. I will repeat that. *Money follows mindset.* Opportunities follow intention. And peace follows vision.

Don't wait to feel wealthy. Practice it now. Practice by valuing your time. Practice by protecting your energy. Practice by saying no to things that drain you. Practice by learning, growing, and choosing better each day.

You don't need a raise to raise your standards. You don't need a big break to break old patterns. You just need to decide that the wealthiest version of you already lives inside you. And that version of you is already building. Already preparing. Already becoming.

I know I said I was closing but I have another thought I would like to share if I may.

Mental wealth means seeing setbacks as setups, not signs of failure. It's the kind of inner strength that won't let you quit on yourself—even when the odds are against you. It's what gives you the courage to say, "I'm not there yet, but I'm on my way."

Mentally wealthy people don't measure progress by popularity or applause. They measure it by peace. They know that real success doesn't always come with confetti. Sometimes it comes with quiet resolve, long nights of self-doubt, yet still choosing to believe in something better.

To be mentally wealthy is to have vision when nothing around you looks like victory. It's planting seeds and trusting that, in time, they'll grow—even when no one claps for you, even when no one is willing to help you water the seed. Doing the work to get the results is not always fun. It's not always flashy. In most cases it's not loud. But once it is harvested, it is powerful. It is said that the mind is a powerful thing to waste but it is also a powerful thing to empower. So, empower your mind with positive growth, cultivating it with knowledge, elevating it with success, strengthen it with perseverance and expanding it with continuous opportunities. I believe that is the key to mental wealth.

Mental wealth allows you to move differently. For example:

- You can see a $20 bill and not have to spend it to feel something.
- You can wear the same clothes and still walk in confidence.
- You can pass on fast money because you're committed to slow, steady freedom.

This kind of mindset makes you dangerous to the system—because you're no longer controlled by the need to prove, to please, or to pretend. Once your mind is free, everything else begins to follow.

This is where the real shift happens—not just in your money, but in your mindset. Not just in your circumstances, but in your character. Not just in your habits, but in your identity.

And here's the final truth that ties it all together: **self-control is the currency of freedom.**

You can't master your money until you master your mind. You can't master your relationships until you learn to master your reactions. You can't build lasting wealth if you're constantly moved by impulse, emotion, or ego.

Self-control isn't about deprivation—it's about direction.

When you develop discipline over your urges, you start living intentionally. You stop letting emotions dictate your actions. You don't buy just because you feel low. You don't lash out because you're angry. You don't settle for toxic relationships because you're lonely. You don't abuse your body because you're tired. You slow down, breathe, and choose wisely.

Every decision becomes a vote for your future.

Self-control touches everything:

- **Money:** You learn to save instead of spending emotionally. You budget. You invest. You wait for the right time.
- **Mind:** You pause before reacting. You replace negative thoughts with truth. You protect your peace.
- **Relationships:** You set boundaries. You walk away from disrespect. You communicate instead of exploding.
- **Health:** You fuel your body, not numb it. You prioritize rest, water, movement. You see yourself as worth the care.

All these areas are connected. If one is out of control, the others suffer. If your mind is chaotic, your money will follow. If your emotions rule you, your health will collapse. If you can't say no, your peace will pay the price.

But when you grow your self-control, everything else aligns. You become powerful. Not because you dominate others, but because you lead yourself. And when you lead yourself with discipline, love, and clarity, you don't just build wealth—you become the foundation of a legacy.

And that my friend is how you transform from survival to strategy and stop living broke.

CHAPTER FOUR
Breaking the Poverty Mindset

The world will shape you if you let it. From the neighborhoods we grow up into the shows we watch and the people we hang around—everything sends messages about who we are, what we deserve, and what's possible. There's a saying, whom ever you associate with is whom you eventually become. So, choose your association wisely. I will discuss this in more depth later in this chapter.

But for now...

If you're trying to come out of a poverty mindset, understand this: it's not just about income—it's about environment. A poverty mindset keeps you stuck even when your circumstances start to change. It whispers lies like, "This is the best you'll ever have," or "People like us don't do things like that." I know, I have had folks tell me that I was doing too much, or I think I'm better than them and the list go on. All because I wanted better than my current circumstance. But because I wanted to be accepted, I digressed and moved the way the mass dictated was suitable behavior for me. I was living so miserable, but they were satisfied.

However, the good news is that my mindset began to change.

May I explain? One of the most powerful ways to change the mindset is to change who—and what—you surround yourself with.

May I continue to be real? You can't grow if you're always the smartest or most motivated person in the room. Comfort may feel safe, but it rarely produces growth. True transformation happens when you place yourself in environments that challenge your thinking and forces you to level up.

You need to be around people who stretch you—individuals whose vision is so bold it shakes you out of your small thinking. People who operate with discipline, creativity, and courage. People who make you question your excuses and inspire you to trade them in for action.

When you surround yourself with greatness, you absorb greatness. Their energy pushes you to raise your standards. Their wisdom teaches you to see life from new perspectives. Their hunger reminds you that settling is never an option.

Growth does not come from standing in the spotlight alone. It comes from being humble enough to learn, hungry enough to keep reaching, and wise enough to seek out networks that make you uncomfortable in the best way possible.

If you want to elevate, you must step into rooms where you are not the ceiling, but the floor—where the people around you pull you higher and push you further than you could ever go alone.

Here's what I learned about leveling up mentally and financially: **proximity is power.**

When I started attending financial podcast, free events, churches, networking events, and even local banks—I met people who talked differently. They didn't just talk about bills; they talked about wealth. They didn't just talk about problems; they talked about plans.

There's a woman named Deborah (I changed the name) changed the way I saw money forever. She was in her 60s, had grown up on welfare, and now owned multiple rental properties. I asked her how she did it. She smiled and said, "I stopped hanging around people who wanted to stay broke." That hit me hard. Because at the time, I was surrounded by people who wanted to complain more than they wanted to change.

*Tip One. The world will keep you small, if you let it.

I remembered once I was invited to a networking event. I almost didn't go. I didn't think I had the right clothes, the right talk, or the right background. But I went and that one night changed everything. I met a man who ran a successful company. He asked me what I did, and I hesitated. But I told him anyway. He looked me in the eye and said, "You're in the people business. That means your potential is limitless—if you know how to use it."

From that day forward, I stopped playing small. I started watching what rich people read. What they listened to. How they talked. What they prioritized. I noticed how they guarded their time, their energy, and their circles and networks. They weren't better than me—they were just operating with a different mindset. And I wanted that.

*Tip Two. Surround yourself with growth

Here's how I recommend that you start surrounding yourself with smarter, richer, more focused people:

1. **Get in the Room** – Look for workshops, panels, community events, webinars, podcasts. You don't need an invitation to grow—just a decision, so decide.

2. **Read Like You're Hungry** – Biographies, business books, mindset resources. Fill your mind with new ideas. The world is too big to stay small, so stop staying small.

3. **Change Your Media Diet** – If you only follow people who make you laugh but not think, you're feeding your comfort—not your calling. Redo your media diet.

4. **Stop Justifying Poverty Mindsets** – Statements like "I don't need all that" or "Money doesn't make you happy" often come from fear or limitation, not truth. Let's be clear money should not be what makes you happy however what you can make money do for you should.

5. **Ask Questions** – The smartest people I've met are also the most curious. You don't have to know everything—you just have to be willing to learn. I heard a preacher say once that he is not a know it all, he is a learn it all. And I have adopted that mindset.

Let me be clear on some things:

You don't have to cut off everyone from your past, but you *do* need to prioritize those who speak to your future. If the world you grew up in taught you to shrink, it's your job now to surround yourself with people who push you to expand. Because here's the truth: the world is wide. And know that mental wealth, financial freedom, mental stability, emotional balance is possible for you. But you have to put yourself in environments where that truth is normal, not rare.

Please do me this huge favor. Take this book into the bathroom or go to a mirror. Look at yourself in the mirror and recite this to yourself. I was not born to play small. I was born to evolve.

Now surround yourself around new like-minded people. Evolution happens faster when you're surrounded by people who see greatness in you—even when you don't yet see it in yourself.

*Tip Three. The 10th Person Principle

I briefly touched on this next part in the beginning of this chapter. Here's a concept that changed my life completely: **you are the average of the people you spend the most time with.**

If you spend time with nine broke, bitter, or negative people—guess what? You'll eventually become the tenth. Not because you're weak, but because energy is contagious. Habits are shared. Conversations shape your perspective.

Now if you spend your time with nine people who are building businesses, investing in themselves, healing, dreaming, growing—and you'll become the tenth. Not by force, but by influence.

Do you get it?

The people around you will either hold you down or lift you higher. Every circle you belong to is shaping your future, whether you realize it or not. Some people reinforce your comfort, keeping you stuck in the same habits, the same excuses, the same cycles that never produce growth. Others challenge you to rise—demanding more from you, stretching your vision, and pushing you into spaces you never thought you could reach.

You're not being disloyal by outgrowing old patterns. Too often, we stay in environments that no longer serve us out of guilt, fear, or the desire to be accepted. But loyalty to dysfunction is not love—it's bondage. True responsibility is choosing to honor your future more than your past. It's having the courage to reshape your thinking, even if it means being misunderstood by those who refuse to change.

That's the essence of the **10th Person Principle**: you were never meant to be the tenth broke person in a line of broke people. You were meant to be the one who breaks the pattern. You are the generational disruptor, the one who proves that poverty, excuses, and mediocrity don't have to be inherited. Someone has to stand up and say, "The cycle ends with me."

Breaking isn't easy—it's uncomfortable, it's lonely at times, and it requires sacrifice. But remember you're not just breaking away from something; you're breaking through to get to something. You're breaking through to get to freedom, to get to opportunity, to get to a future where your children and their children see a new standard of life.

So, get to breaking. Break the excuses. Break the generational mindset that told you struggle is normal. Break the belief that you must accept less than what you deserve. Break the pattern of being the 10th person and become the 1st person—the one who changes everything.

*Tip Four. Breaking Broke Habits

Here's another truth that might sting before it sets you free: **broke habits are what keep people broke.**

Changing your financial life means changing your entire life—how you think, how you eat, how you sleep, who you trust, how you spend time (notice I didn't say your time), and how you react when things go wrong.

Ask yourself:

- Are you sleeping until noon, then wondering why you feel behind?
- Are you scrolling for hours but "don't have time" to budget?
- Are you overeating or emotionally spending when life gets hard?
- Are you holding onto toxic relationships out of fear or convenience?
- Are you ignoring your health because you feel powerless in other areas?

These aren't just lifestyle issues—they are also wealth issues.

Success requires structure, routine, discipline, and vision. Every time you choose structure over chaos, you build stability. Every time you say no to temptation, you are saying yes to your financial freedom future. So do yourself this favor that I found works for me:

Wake up earlier.

Drink more water.

Journal your goals.

Walk away from drama.

Say no when your spirit is tired.

In essence take care of you. Put you first. Too often, people tie their destiny to external rewards—waiting for a raise, a promotion, or some external validation before they decide to take life seriously. They believe success is something handed to them by someone else's decision, rather than something they create through their own growth.

But your future doesn't begin with a new title, a bigger paycheck, or someone else finally recognizing your worth.

Your future begins the moment you decide to become a better version of yourself. It starts when you commit to healing from past pain instead of carrying it into every new opportunity. It deepens when you choose focus over distraction, discipline over comfort, and bold action over hesitation.

Your next season isn't about waiting—it's about becoming. Opportunities expand when you do. Doors open when you are prepared to walk through them. The life you dream about is connected to the version of you that refuses to stay the same.

Your future isn't just waiting on a promotion. It's waiting on the healed, focused, bold version of you to make better choices now.

*Tip Five. Let Go of the Past

But there's something else you have to do—and it's just as important as budgeting, reading, or changing your circles in networks:

You have to tell yourself—daily—that your past is behind you. And that you are worthy of a bright future.

No matter what mistakes you've made. No matter how many times you've failed. You are not your past. You can't drive forward while staring in the rearview mirror. **Regret is not a growth strategy. Shame is not a success plan.**

You've got to reprogram your inner voice every day, and remind yourself:

- I am not my debt.
- I am not my environment.
- I am not my failures.
- I am not what I lacked—I am what I choose to build.

Your future doesn't care who hurt you, who doubted you, or who walked away. It isn't sitting around replaying your past disappointments. It's waiting for you to decide whether you will rise above them. The truth is, your future is neutral—it will give you whatever you're prepared to work for, believe in, and build toward.

What your future *does* care about is whether you believe you are worthy of healing. Because broken thinking creates broken habits, and broken habits create broke living. If you never deal with the pain, the fear, or the lies you've told yourself, you'll keep repeating the same financial and personal cycles. Healing clears the space for growth. It allows you to think bigger, plan smarter, and chase opportunities with clarity instead of desperation.

Your future also cares about whether you rise to the occasion. Life will keep presenting you with chances— chances to learn, chances to save, chances to invest, chances to change your mindset. But if you shrink back every time it feels uncomfortable, you'll stay stuck in the same financial struggles you've always known. Rising to the occasion doesn't mean you won't be afraid—it means you move forward *in spite* of the fear because you know staying broke is a far worse option.

The future you desire—the one filled with positive, productive, lucrative results—doesn't arrive by accident. It's built choice by choice, day by day. It's created when you stop rehearsing who left you and start rehearsing the vision of where you're going. It's secured when you stop trying to prove your doubters wrong and start proving yourself right.

So, stop concentrating on the past and focus on the future and know that:

You are not too late.
You are not too far gone.
You are not too broken.

You are worthy.
You are ready.
You are rising.

The question is simple: will you live in the story of who hurt you, or will you write a new story of healing, growth, and financial freedom? Because your future is waiting— and it's only going to manifest the version of you that you decide-rather that is continuing down an unhealthy mental and unstable financial path or you finally decides to stop living broke.

CHAPTER FIVE
Designing a Life of Joy, Wealth and Purpose and Legacy

There comes a point in your journey where you should stop surviving and start building. You begin to realize that your life—your health, your finances, your peace—isn't something that just happens to you. It's something you *design* on purpose.

After all the reflection, the strategy, the unlearning, and the healing, Chapter Five is where it becomes clear: **you are the architect of your own future.**

No more waiting for permission.
No more looking back in regret.
No more rehearsing old pain.

This chapter is about designing a life that feels good on the *inside*—not just looks good on the outside. It's about your real true happiness.

But What Does Happiness Really Look Like?

We've been taught to equate happiness with success, and success with money, and money with more. But real happiness? It's simpler—and richer—than that.

I believe that real happiness is:

- Waking up and not dreading the day.
- Having the freedom to say no.
- Being at peace with who you are.
- Doing work that lights your soul.
- Resting without guilt.

For others it may be more or something else altogether. No matter how you define happiness know that it is not a destination. It's a design. It's created through daily habits, honest choices, and courageous vision.

Vision Is a Muscle

If you want to change your life, you have to start by seeing a better one. And if you can't see it yet, that's okay—vision is a muscle. The more you use it, the stronger it gets. My sister shared a saying she heard, "When the mind is blind the eyes can't see."

Interesting. Ponder on that for a moment.

I want you to take out a notebook and write it all down:

- What does your day looks like?/What does your ideal day look like?
- Where do you live?/ Where do you want to live?
- How do you earn money?/How do you want to earn your money?
- Who are you surrounded by?/Who do you want to be surrounded by?
- How do you feel when you wake up?/How do you want to feel when you wake up?
- What is it that your mind sees?/What do you want your mind to see?

Be truthful with yourself so that your life can began to rise to the level of your expectations. If you expect struggle, you'll settle for survival. But if you expect joy, peace, abundance, and purpose—you'll begin to make choices that align with that expectation. It's just that simple. But simple isn't always easy for the blind minded person.

The Power of Goals + Grit

Now that you know what you want, it's time to build a plan. A goal without a plan is nothing more than a wish— a dream you hope for but never see. Wishes don't change your bank account, your health, or your mindset. Plans do.

Start simple. Choose one financial goal, one health goal, and one personal growth goal. Don't overwhelm yourself with ten different targets. Focus on the three areas that shape the quality of your life and the strength of your future.

Then, break each goal into small, repeatable steps. Consistency beats intensity. It's not about doing everything at once—it's about doing the right things daily until they become second nature. Pay off a little debt each month. Walk for twenty minutes a day. Read ten pages of a book that challenges your thinking. Small actions, stacked over time, build big results.

Don't wait for perfect timing, because perfection is a trap. Waiting until you feel ready or until conditions are ideal will keep you stuck. Progress, not perfection, is the fuel of transformation. Every step forward, no matter how small, is proof that you refuse to live broke—in your finances, in your health, or in your growth.

The power of goals lies in progression. When you focus on moving forward, lack of perfection is no longer an excuse. You stop saying, "One day," and start living, "Day one." That's how you create momentum, and momentum is what breaks the cycle of living broke.

Grit is not glamorous. It's doing the boring thing again and again until it finally produces results. It's choosing consistency over excitement, showing up even when no one notices, and refusing to quit when applause is absent. Grit is the fuel that keeps you moving when the emotions fade, when progress feels slow, and when the reward is still miles away.

Most people quit in the silence. They want the quick win, the fast money, the instant recognition. But wealth—whether financial, emotional, or spiritual—is rarely built that way. Real success is created in quiet seasons when no one is watching. It's built in the late nights when you're paying off debt dollar by dollar. It's built in the early mornings when you're reading, planning, or exercising while others sleep. It's built in the discipline of repeating small steps until they become unshakable habits.

That's how dreams are built: in silence, in steps, in seasons. Silence, because greatness grows in the unseen before it is celebrated in the open. Steps, because progress comes one choice at a time, stacked patiently over days, months, and years. Seasons, because there will be times of planting, waiting, and harvesting—and you cannot skip the process.

I have a friend, let's call her Bella. She was drowning in $50,000 of credit card debt. At first, she wanted a miracle—some big break that would erase it all. But when the miracle didn't come, and everyone she asked, including me, was not able to help her, she chose grit. She built a simple plan: cut unnecessary spending, work a few extra hours, and pay off a set amount every month. For the first year, it felt like nothing was happening. No one clapped when she said no to dinner outings. No one praised her when she picked up a side hustle on weekends.

But in silence, she chipped away. Month after month, her balance dropped. After three years of steady, boring grit, Lisa was debt-free. That quiet discipline gave her the confidence and freedom to start investing—something she never thought possible when she was broke.

Here's the deal. If you want to stop living broke, you must embrace the grind that no one praises. You must be willing to invest in yourself long before the results show. Grit will ask you to commit when motivation fades, to trust the process when the outcome seems invisible, and to keep building even when your present looks nothing like the future you're chasing.

The truth is that dreams don't come alive in the spotlight. They are forged in the unseen discipline of grit and that is how you become boss over your life.

What It Means to Be the B.O.S.S.

Now let's talk about control. **Real control.** Being the B.O.S.S. of your life means more than shouting "I'm in charge!" It means embodying a mindset of strength, focus, and responsibility. It's not about dominating others—it's about developing yourself so deeply that leadership becomes a natural outcome.

For me, B.O.S.S. stands for:

- **B**old
- **O**ptimistic
- **S**ervanthood
- **S**uccess

Let's break this down—*really* break it down:

BOLD means you speak up for yourself even when your voice shakes. It means taking risks that make your knees wobble because what the future *you* want is worth it. Boldness is setting boundaries even if others don't like them. It's making that phone call, launching that idea, walking away from toxicity. Boldness is how you declare war on mediocrity. Bold is choosing you and what's best for you FIRST.

OPTIMISTIC doesn't mean being blindly positive. It means choosing hope, especially when your past tried to convince you there's none. It's looking at your bank account, your relationship, your past trauma—and still saying, "I'm not done yet." Optimism is power because it fuels action. Pessimism paralyzes, but optimism moves you forward.

SERVANTHOOD is where humility meets leadership. You don't have to be loud to be powerful. You don't have to dominate to lead. You lift others as you climb. You use your growth not as a crown, but as a bridge. Being a servant doesn't make you small—it makes you unforgettable. It's the most magnetic form of leadership.

SUCCESS is the fruit of the first three. But real success isn't just about what you gain—it's about what you become. It's the freedom to live your truth. It's alignment between who you are and how you live. It's the ability to sleep peacefully, love openly, give generously, and wake up excited about your day.

This is what B.O.S.S. means to me. And for me operating in B.O.S.S.-hood means that you:

- Control your emotions before you try to lead others.

- Structure your days around purpose, not just convenience.
- Choose hard conversations over silent resentment.
- Plan your money instead of letting it control you.
- Act with character, even when no one is watching.

You can't lead the world around you if you haven't first learned how to lead yourself. True leadership begins within. Before you can influence others, manage a team, or run a business, you must first master the discipline of directing your own choices, your own mindset, and your own actions.

So, when you say you're the boss of your life, don't just wear it like a title—walk it like a lifestyle. Being a B.O.S.S. means taking ownership of your decisions, setting your own standards, and refusing to let excuses dictate your destiny. It's not about arrogance or control over others—it's about accountability and discipline with yourself.

You were never meant to follow the crowd. You were created to set the tone, to be the example that others can look to when they wonder what strength, resilience, and responsibility look like in action. And the beautiful truth is this: everyone has the ability to be a B.O.S.S. You don't have to be bossy over someone else or compete to be the "head boss." The assignment is not to control and dominate others—it's to control yourself.

So, concentrate on B.O.S.S.ing yourself—your mindset, your money, your growth, and your future. Because when you take charge of you, everything else begins to shift. There's an old song that says, *"Walk like an Egyptian."* I say, **walk like a B.O.S.S.**

Now that you are walking like a B.O.S.S, let's discuss financial freedom and a rich life.

Financial freedom is powerful—but **it's not everything.** It is, however, the gateway to a richer, fuller life when used with wisdom and heart. True financial freedom means you no longer live at the mercy of bills, jobs you hate, or constant anxiety about emergencies. It means being able to give, travel, rest, invest, and serve without sacrificing your health or peace. Seems simple enough, but it's more than that. It's also about being *available*—to your purpose, to your family, to the people who need you most. Let's discuss that word for a moment. Availability. I want to share a story with you.

When I was working a traditional job as a manager, I thought I had stability. I followed the rules, scheduled my time carefully, and relied on my PTO to create balance between work and life. One year, I took some time off to go home for an important event. It was a meaningful trip, but it came with a cost—I had used up the little time I was allowed.

Not long after, life happened. A family situation arose that demanded my presence. My heart told me to go, but my job—and the restrictions of my paycheck—said otherwise. I couldn't be there physically. Instead, I had to offer comfort and support over the phone. Although I made myself available via phone, my physical presence was warranted. And although everyone said they understood, it placed a sour taste in my then current life's financial position.

That moment opened my eyes. I realized how easily a job and lack of money could dictate my availability, even for the people and moments that mattered most. And it didn't stop there. A few more situations came and went—birthdays, milestones, emotional gatherings—and each time I was reminded that I wasn't in control. My life was being scheduled by someone else's system. I was living broke.

Now, I understand that in life there will always be times when you simply cannot be everywhere or do everything. That's reality. But there is a difference between natural limitations and financial limitations. Not having the freedom to be available isn't just inconvenient—it's a liability. It's one of the hidden costs of living broke. The moral of this story is that: **My financial status did not allow me the freedom to be available.**

Here is another important tip. **Place yourself in a legal financial position that will allow you to live your life in a way that you can be available for whatever it is that you want to be available for.**

Now let's move on.

When you're financially free, everything shifts. You stop making decisions out of desperation and start making them from vision. You stop living in survival mode and start living in strategy. No longer are you scrambling to cover the basics—you're planning, investing, and positioning yourself for growth. That shift in perspective is priceless.

One of the greatest lessons you will ever learn is how to separate your self-worth from your net worth. Too many people measure their value by what's in their bank account, the kind of car they drive, or the labels on their clothes. But none of those things define who you truly are. They are possessions, not identity.

Your joy must come from who you are, not what you own. When you root your worth in money or material things, you will always be chasing—chasing the next check, the next purchase, the next upgrade. And the dangerous part is, that chase never ends. There will always be someone with more. There will always be a higher level to reach.

That constant pursuit keeps you running but never arriving.

And here's the truth: money, by itself, doesn't make you free. If your happiness, confidence, and sense of value are tied to wealth alone, then you're not free—you're dependent. You've simply traded one form of bondage for another. Financial freedom is powerful, yes, but true freedom is internal. It's knowing that even if every dollar disappeared, your worth would remain untouched.

That doesn't mean money isn't important. It is—it pays bills, provides opportunities, and creates options. But money was designed to be a servant, not a master. When you shift your perspective, you stop obsessing over what you don't have and start building from a place of security within yourself. That's the real secret to breaking the cycle of living broke: mastering money without letting money master you.

Let money be a tool—not your identity. Let it serve you, not enslave you.

But here's what most people miss: financial freedom is not the same as fulfillment. You can be wealthy and still feel empty. You can be debt-free and still be bound—bound by fear, bound by ego, bound by insecurity. The external freedom of money doesn't automatically solve the internal struggles of the heart. That's why so many people with money still feel restless, unfulfilled, or chained to the same unhealthy cycles as before.

Money by itself cannot heal, cannot bring purpose, and cannot give peace. What money can do is magnify who you already are. If you are disciplined, money will amplify that discipline. If you are reckless, money will magnify that recklessness. If you are insecure, money won't cure it—it will only give you bigger, more expensive ways to hide it.

This is why it is not enough to *make* money—you must master money. If you don't, you'll end up on a hamster wheel: running faster, earning more, spending more, and never actually getting ahead. That's what happens when money controls you instead of you controlling it. The paychecks grow, but the cycle stays the same. You may no longer be broke on paper, but you're still broke in mindset—forever chasing and never arriving.

Mastering money means putting it in its rightful place: a tool, not a master. It means learning how to budget, save, invest, and give without being controlled by fear or greed. It means building systems that work for you so you're no longer running in circles but moving forward with clarity and confidence. Because at the end of the day, financial freedom without money mastery is just another version of bondage—one that looks successful on the outside but still feels empty on the inside.

Once you begin mastering money, you'll notice a shift in every part of your life:

- You'll walk with confidence.
- You'll lead with clarity.
- You'll give without guilt.
- You'll plan with purpose.
- You'll say no when appropriate or necessary without feeling guilt.

- You'll stop fighting just to survive—and finally have the space to *live*.

Use your freedom to serve others but never tie your happiness to how much you earn. Remember: the richest life is not one filled with things—it's one filled with peace, legacy, and purpose. At least that is what I believe.

So, build the kind of wealth that money can't buy. Because true richness starts within. I cannot say this enough: It's a *tool*, not your *identity*. Yes, money gives you options. But it doesn't define your worth.

True wealth includes:

- Peace when the bills are paid.
- Joy that doesn't depend on your balance.
- Generosity that isn't driven by guilt.

It's okay to use your financial growth to build the life you love. That's the reward of discipline—enjoying the fruit of your labor without guilt. But it's also powerful to use that growth to lift others, as long as you don't drain yourself in the process. Generosity should flow from overflow, not from empty sacrifice that leaves you broke again.

Still, financial growth is only one part of the story. Money is a tool, but legacy is the true goal. When people remember you, they won't just recall how much money you left behind. They'll remember the lessons you taught, the values you lived by, and the examples you set.

Leaving a legacy means passing down more than wealth— it means passing down wisdom. Teach your children and those you influence how to handle money with responsibility, how to live with integrity, and how to prioritize what truly matters. Leave behind resilience, discipline, generosity, and vision. These are qualities that outlast dollar signs. Because money alone can vanish. It can be spent, lost, or mismanaged. But the principles you model—like self-control, hard work, faith, kindness, and courage—become the true inheritance. They shape generations long after the money is gone.

So yes, use your financial growth to build the life you love. Enjoy it, share it, multiply it. But never forget: the most valuable legacy you can leave is not just in your bank account—it's in the minds, hearts, and habits of those who come after you.

Did you know your legacy begins now not after you die?

Your transformation will not stop with you. It will ripple out. The choices you make today—how you think, spend, love, lead, and live—are laying the foundation for those who come after you. You are teaching the next generation to be winners, not survivors. Builders, not victims. Visionaries, not wanderers.

And when you finally reach that place of freedom, peace, and purpose, you'll realize the greatest gift of all is that you now have the power to lift others—and it is not from a place of exhaustion, but from a place of abundance. Isn't that wonderful? To be able to help others not go down the same path you did just by sharing your wisdom. At least I think it is.

Financial freedom isn't just about having more—it's about becoming more. True freedom transforms you from the inside out. It makes you more grounded, because you're no longer tossed around by financial anxiety. It makes you more generous, because you understand that abundance isn't meant to stop with you—it's meant to flow through you. And it makes you more available, giving you the space and time to show up for the people and causes that matter most to you.

But here's the secret: the real joy of financial freedom doesn't come from the numbers in your account or the possessions you accumulate. Joy flows from a spirit that is whole, secure, and at peace. Without that, all the money in the world still leaves you empty.

That's why the pursuit of freedom must go deeper than wealth. It's about building character while you build your bank account. It's about aligning your career with your calling so that your work carries meaning. It's about showing yourself grace as you grow, refusing to be trapped by perfection or comparison.

So, live richly.
Not just in your wallet, but in your character.

Not just in your career, but in your calling.

Not just in your goals, but in your grace.

This is your legacy. This is your new beginning. You've taken back the wheel—now drive like the world is waiting. Because it is. And if you're still wondering whether you're ready—let me assure you: you are.

You are ready to shed the labels the world tried to put on you. You are ready to break the cycles you were never meant to repeat. You are ready to build wealth that empowers—not impresses. You are ready to be a light in dark places.

This is more than a mindset shift—it's a soul shift. You're not just surviving anymore. You're thriving, healing, leading, and leaving a blueprint behind.

So, when doubt creeps in—and it will—remember: your progress is proof that change is possible. Your story is the evidence that transformation is real. Let hope be your fuel. Let healing be your banner. Let boldness be your peace. You are not alone. You are not too late. You are not too broken. You are exactly where you need to be to take the next step forward. So, take it.

Take it like your life depends on it—because it does. Take it for the version of you that almost gave up. Take it for your children, your legacy, and the people who need to see it done. Take it because being stuck is no longer your story. You are not here by accident. You are reading this at the exact time you were supposed to. This is not just a book—it's a mirror, a call, a shift. And it's your turn now.

So, rise up. Shake the dust off your dreams. Look in the mirror and remind yourself: "I am powerful. I am worthy. I am enough."

You're not broken—you're being rebuilt. You're not late—you're right on time. You're not lost—you're discovering a new path. And as long as you have breath, you still have power. Power to rewrite your story. Power to take ownership of your future. Power to walk like you've already won. You've cried long enough. You've waited long enough. You've doubted long enough. It's time. Now take it. And never look back because you deserve to Stop Living Broke!

Epilogue: Your Freedom Starts Now

If there's one thing I hope you take from this journey, it's this: change begins the moment you decide to stop handing your power over to your past. The cycles you've seen, the struggles you've endured, the mistakes you've made— they do not define your future. What defines your future is the choice you make right now to rise, to take ownership, and to build differently.

You have always had the ability to lead your life. The truth is, the power was never lost—it was only buried beneath fear, habits, and limiting beliefs. But now, you have the tools to uncover it. You know that financial freedom is not just about numbers in a bank account—it's about mindset, awareness, consistency, and courage.

Your story matters. Your voice matters. Your future is calling. And it's calling you to live free—free from broke thinking, free from cycles of debt and fear, free from silence and shame.

Take control. Stay the course. Keep learning. Keep building. Every small decision matters. Every step forward counts. Don't wait for perfect conditions—they don't exist. Don't wait for someone else to come and rescue you—they won't. You are not powerless.

No one else can take back the wheel for you. But now, you don't need them to. You are the driver. You are the mapmaker. You are the architect of your life.

And here's the good news: your best days are not behind you—they are ahead of you. Your future is rich with possibility. Your legacy is waiting to be written. And your freedom begins the moment you decide, once and for all, to stop living broke.

Your Final Declaration

Say this out loud and mean it:

"Today, I choose to stop living broke. I choose to live free, live wisely, and live richly—not just in my wallet, but in my mind, my habits, and my future. I am the driver of my destiny. My freedom starts now."

About the Author

Dr. JoeDrell Benjamin, known to most as **Sista Jay Jay**, is a remarkable woman whose life journey embodies resilience, redemption, and relentless determination. Once an ex-felon, she refused to let her past define her future. Instead, she transformed her struggles into steppingstones, rewriting her story into one of victory and purpose.

Today, Sista Jay Jay wears many hats—and wears them well. She is a proud mother, filmmaker, actor, business owner, mentor, acting coach, podcaster, publisher, and author. Each role reflects her creativity, drive, and commitment to building platforms that uplift others. Her deep love for the arts, sports and her passion for helping people fuel her mission to make a lasting impact in both personal and professional spaces.

As a woman of faith, her relationship with God serves as the foundation of everything she does. That faith, coupled with her boldness, keeps her grounded while guiding her vision. Her signature motto, *"Collaboration over competition. Individually grinding together"* captures her belief in the power of unity, community, and shared success. She reminds others that "individually grinding together equals a win for everyone," encouraging people to drop the mindset of scarcity and embrace the beauty of collective growth.

What makes Sista Jay Jay so dynamic is her ability to inspire through both her words and her work. Whether she's on set directing a film, mentoring a young actor, coaching someone through life's challenges, publishing a book, co-hosting or hosting her podcast, she leads with authenticity. She doesn't just talk about transformation— she lives it. Her story is living proof that with vision, faith, and determination, anyone can rise above their circumstances and create a future filled with possibility.

Her influence continues to expand across multiple industries, but her greatest impact is in the lives she touches daily. She embodies what it means to live boldly, to stand in your truth, and to use every gift you've been given to serve others.

You can follow and connect with Sista Jay Jay across all social media platforms at I Am Sista Jay Jay or on her website at www.iamsistajayjay.com, because her journey isn't just about her, it's about showing others that transformation, empowerment, and success are within reach for anyone willing to believe and put in the work.

Also, visit R.A.G Girl Publishing, home to Sista Jay Jay's books and the works of over 200 collaborating authors across a wide range of genres—fiction, self-help, children's stories, poetry, memoirs, and motivational guides. There's truly something for every reader. Explore the collection and purchase your copies today at www.raggirlpublishing.com.

Sista Jay Jay (Dr. JoeDrell Benjamin)

www.ingramcontent.com/pod-product-compliance
Lightning Source LLC
Chambersburg PA
CBHW070056100426

42740CB00013B/2850